...t I was free, and they should be free.
-Harriet Tubman

I am not afraid... I was born to do this
-Joan of Arc

I am a queen. And as long as I live, I will reign.
-Zenobia

To create one's world in any of the arts takes courage.
-Georgia O'Keeffe

...what ...rence ...ning is ...trees.
...a Woodhull

...side of the room and the guys on the other side of the room. I guess they didn't want to associate with me. But I could hold my own with them and sometimes did better.
-Mary Golda Ross

A woman is like a tea bag. You can't tell how strong she is until you put her in hot water.
-Eleanor Roosevelt

HISTORY'S YEARBOOK

VIRGINIA LOH-HAGAN

GIRL LEADERS

The world has used me so unkindly. I fear it has made me suspicious of everyone.
-Mary Anning

Liberty!
–Inayat Khan's last word

If you hold your hand closed, nothing good can come in. The open hand is blessed, for it gives in abundance, even as it receives.
-Biddy Mason

I've never been afraid in my life.
-Nancy Wake

I attribute my success to this: I never gave or took any excuse.
–Florence Nightingale

Women should be someone, and not something.
–Mary Cassatt

Well-behaved women seldom make history.
-Laurel Thatcher Ulrich

...Here is the day. We must welcome it with song.
–Marie Laveau

The title of Queen rang sweet to my ears.
-Catherine the Great

I0896418

Contents

Introduction

We are celebrating girl leaders. Leaders take charge. They're trailblazers. Trailblazers make things happen. They do things first. They do things in a new way.

Girl leaders include rulers. They include **politicians.** Politicians serve the government. They run in elections. Elections are when people vote for representatives.

But it's not easy being a girl leader. Some people think that women shouldn't lead.

Throughout history, women have shown that they're tough. They're smart. They're strong. The girl leaders in this book rise to the top. They paved the way for today's girl leaders. You don't have to lead a nation or a business to be a leader. You can still be a leader. Speak up. Go after what you want. But also take time to listen to others. Be a problem solver.

Here's to you and all the girl leaders in our lives!

chapter 1

BEST ALL-AROUND

Queen Elizabeth I

> Though the sex to which I belong is considered weak, you will nevertheless find me a rock that bends to no wind. – **Queen Elizabeth I**

The "Best All-Around" award goes to Elizabeth I. Elizabeth I lived from 1533 to 1603. She was Queen of England and Ireland. She never married. She said she was married to her country. Her rule was called the Golden Age.

She was one of the most powerful rulers ever. She defeated the Spanish army. She changed England for the better. She brought peace. She expanded England by exploring other lands.

She also supported the arts. She loved clothes. She loved plays. She loved dances. She spoke several languages. She was educated. She was also athletic. She hunted. She rode horses. She did it all!

chapter 2

MOST DIPLOMATIC

Nanye'hi

> Our cry is all for peace. Let it continue. This peace must last forever. Let your women's sons be ours. Our sons be yours. Let your women hear our words. –Nanye'hi

The "Most **Diplomatic**" award goes to Nanye'hi. Diplomats solve problems. Nanye-hi was Cherokee. Cherokees are Native American people. She was the "Beloved Woman." This was a powerful position. She led the Women's **Council**. She was also on the Council of Chiefs. Council means a group of leaders.

In the late 1700s, she made peace between Native Americans and white settlers. She'd warn settlers against attacks. She knew Cherokees couldn't win against the white settlers. She pushed for everyone to live together in peace.

She also fought for Cherokees to keep their lands. She introduced dairy products and weaving to the Cherokees. She wanted them to **adapt** to the new world. Adapt means change.

chapter 3

MOST PERSUASIVE

Princess Pingyang

> She was no ordinary woman.
>
> –Princess Pingyang's father

The "Most **Persuasive**" award goes to Princess Pingyang. Persuade means to convince others to do things. Pingyang was born between 598 and 600 CE in China. She persuaded 70,000 people to join her army. First, she fed hungry people. She won their loyalty. Then she went to different towns. People liked her. They followed her. Pingyang had strict rules. She didn't let soldiers steal. She didn't let them hurt women and children.

She was a **warrior**. Warrior means fighter. Her army was called the Army of the Lady. Pingyang took over the government. She made her father an **emperor**. Emperors are rulers. Pingyang started the Tang **Dynasty**. Dynasty means a ruling family.

chapter 4

MOST SUPPORTIVE

Queen Charlotte

> Oh! What a blessing to keep good company!
>
> –Queen Charlotte

The "Most Supportive" award goes to Queen Charlotte. In 1761, she married King George III. She became Queen of Great Britain and Ireland. She may be England's first **biracial** queen. Biracial means belonging to two races. Many historians believe she had black relatives in her family line.

Charlotte supported artists and musicians. She supported the works of famous **composers**. Composers write music. She helped Wolfgang Amadeus Mozart. Charlotte and Mozart sang a song together. Mozart dedicated songs to her.

Charlotte loved plants. She was the first to set up a Christmas tree in her castle. She helped grow Kew Gardens in London. Explorers gave her plants from other lands. Charlotte kept these plants in her gardens. They became part of the Kew Gardens. Today, the garden houses some of the most diverse plants in the world. Diverse means different.

chapter 5

MOST ATHLETIC

Eleanor Roosevelt

> A woman is like a tea bag. You can't tell how strong she is until you put her in hot water.
>
> –Eleanor Roosevelt

The "Most Athletic" award goes to Eleanor Roosevelt. Roosevelt was the First Lady of the United States. First Lady is the title of a male president's wife. She served from 1933 to 1945. She was one of the tallest first ladies in U.S. history. She did so many great things. She fought for justice. She fought for human rights. She helped people get jobs. She also took care of herself.

She did calisthenics to radio music. Calisthenics are exercises. They include stretching, pulling, pushing, and jogging in place. She did this every morning.

She also rode horses. Her favorite horse was named Dot. Roosevelt did other sports. She loved swimming. She loved dancing. She loved shooting at targets. She loved playing field hockey in school.

chapter 6

MOST DETERMINED

Catherine the Great

> The title of Queen rang sweet to my ears.
>
> –Catherine the Great

The "Most **Determined**" award goes to Catherine the Great. Determined means never giving up on goals. Catherine the Great ruled Russia from 1762 to 1796. She was Russia's longest-ruling female.

Catherine married Peter III. He was next in line to rule Russia. She was determined to rule. She helped get Peter arrested. He gave his power to Catherine. He was killed by someone Catherine knew. Some people think Catherine planned his death.

She was determined to be a good ruler. She added land to Russia. She wrote many books. She wanted to improve Russia's education system. She wanted to improve the government. She supported the arts. She made Russia into a world power.

chapter 7

MOST TALENTED

Queen Liliuokalani

> The acquisition of knowledge has been a passion with me during my whole life.
>
> –Queen Liliuokalani

The "Most Talented" award goes to Liliuokalani. Liliuokalani was the last ruler of Hawaii. She was Hawaii's first female ruler. But she didn't rule for very long. The U.S. government took control of Hawaii. Liliuokalani fought for a free Hawaii. She wanted to take back her power. But this caused problems. She didn't want war. So, she gave up Hawaii.

She was talented. She was a poet. She was musical. She wrote over 160 songs. She wrote "Aloha Oe." She wrote this song in 1878. This song means "Farewell to Thee." It's a famous Hawaiian song.

chapter 8

GO-GETTER

Cleopatra

> I will not be triumphed over.
>
> –Cleopatra

The "Go-Getter" award goes to Cleopatra VII. Cleopatra was Queen of Egypt. Her country loved her. She knew many languages. She ruled during the 1st century BCE. She cared for her country. She focused on her goals. She was a strong leader. She was also Egypt's last ruling leader.

She ruled with her brother. But this didn't last long. Her brother wanted to rule alone. He exiled her. Exile means to force out. This didn't stop Cleopatra. She raised an army. She also gained the trust of Julius Caesar. Caesar was a powerful man in Rome. He helped her regain the throne of Egypt.

Caesar was killed. Cleopatra partnered with another powerful Roman man. His name was Marc Antony. This partnership caused a war. It ended in both their deaths.

Cleopatra's life didn't end well. But she was a smart ruler. She was persuasive. She adapted to her situations.

chapter 9

HEART OF GOLD

Eva Perón

I am only a simple woman who lives to serve Perón and my people. –Eva Perón

The "Heart of Gold" award goes to Eva Perón. Perón was Argentina's First Lady. She was called Evita. People loved her. Perón was active in politics. She helped her husband get elected. She led the offices for health and **labor**. Labor means work.

Perón created her own charity. Charities are organizations that help the needy. Her charity raised money. The money helped poor and sick people. The money helped start hospitals. It opened schools. It opened homes for **orphans** and older people. Orphans are children without parents. She even helped women get the right to vote.

chapter 10

MOST INVOLVED

Shirley Chisholm

> I am the candidate of the people. And my presence before you now symbolizes a new era in American political history.
>
> **–Shirley Chisholm**

The "Most Involved" award goes to Shirley Chisholm. Chisholm was the first African American woman to be elected to the U.S. Congress. This happened in 1968. She was also the first African American to run for U.S. president. She fought for equal rights. She fought for education.

She lived in Barbados. She got a British education. She went to a one-room schoolhouse. She moved back to the United States. She graduated from Brooklyn College. She won prizes for her debating skills. She got a master's degree from Columbia University. She studied education. She became a teacher. She directed a child care center. She taught at Mount Holyoke College. She spoke at colleges across the country.

chapter 11

MOST COURAGEOUS

Benazir Bhutto

> The government I led gave ordinary people peace, security, dignity, and opportunity to progress.
>
> –Benazir Bhutto

The "Most Courageous" award goes to Benazir Bhutto. Her first name means "one without equal." She was born in 1953. She was the **prime minister** of Pakistan. Prime minister means the top leader. She was the youngest prime minister in Pakistan. She was the first woman elected to lead a Muslim country. She faced a lot of hate. Some people thought she was taking a man's job.

She was smart. She graduated from Harvard College in Massachusetts. She also studied at Oxford University in the United Kingdom.

She was courageous. She fought against military rule. She wanted what was best for her country. She wanted to end censorship in the media. Censorship is the practice of banning certain writings or works. She gave electricity to over 21,000 poor villages. She wanted everyone to be educated. She promoted women's rights. She faced a lot of hardship.

chapter 12

LIFE OF THE PARTY

Marie Antoinette

I also had friends ... Let them know that, to my last moment, I was thinking of them. –Marie Antoinette

The "Life of the Party" award goes to Marie Antoinette. She was born into a rich, royal family. She married into another rich, royal family. She married Louis XVI in 1770. She was the last Queen of France.

She was very social. She loved playing games. She loved wearing fancy clothes. She loved to party.

She spent a lot of money. For example, she built a farm on palace land. This was so she and her friends could pretend to be farmers.

The French people blamed her for their money troubles. Marie Antoinette was killed in 1793. She had the option of escaping. But she stood by her family.

Top Memories

- **2500 to 2330 BCE:** Kubaba ruled Sumeria. Sumeria is now called Iraq. Kubaba was the first girl leader in history. Her name was found on a clay tablet called the "King List." Her kingship passed on to her son. After she died, people still honored Kubaba as a goddess.
- **July 21, 1960:** Sirimavo Bandaranaike became prime minister of Sri Lanka. She was the world's first elected female head of government. Sri Lanka is an island country. It's in South Asia. It's in the Indian Ocean.
- **1964:** Patsy Mink was from Hawaii. She was elected to the U.S. Congress. She was the first Asian American to do so. She was also the first woman of color to do so. She helped pass many bills supporting equal rights and education.
- **2005:** Ellen Johnson Sirleaf was elected president of Liberia. This made her the first elected female leader in Africa. She won a Nobel Peace Prize in 2011. She supported women's rights.

Advice from the Field

Margaret Thatcher lived from 1925 to 2013. She was the prime minister of Great Britain. She was Britain's first female prime minister. She was also Europe's first female prime minister. She was the only prime minister in the 20th century to win 3 terms in a row. She was called the Iron Lady. She was tough. She was strong. She was determined. She was determined to make changes. She made decisions even if people didn't like her. She did what she thought was right for her country. Her advice was to be uncompromising. Uncompromising means to not give in to others' demands. It means to not give up on your beliefs. She said, "If you just set out to be liked, you would be prepared to compromise on anything at any time. And you would achieve nothing." She also said, "Don't follow the crowd. Let the crowd follow you."

Student Life & Clubs

Are you interested in being a leader? Consider the Junior State of America (JSA). Its goal is to help high school students gain leadership skills. Another goal is to help youth become better citizens and debaters. Debaters are people who argue about important issues. To win elections, politicians must debate. Debating is a great skill for future leaders. The JSA is organized by students. It has local, regional, and state chapters. Chapters are smaller groups. JSA members elect their own leaders. They organize meetings and events. They organize a summer program. They meet other students from other cities. JSA started in 1934. It was started by Professor E. A. Rogers. Over 500,000 student members have participated. JSA has famous alumni. Alumni are graduates of a program. Tom Brady of the New England Patriots was a JSA member.

"Well-behaved women seldom make history."

–Laurel Thatcher Ulrich

Did You Know...

- October 11 is the International Day of the Girl. It started in 2012. The goal of the day is to support more opportunities for girls. Many events are hosted on this day. They learn about what it is like to be a leader.
- Rebecca Felton was from Georgia. She was the first woman in the U.S. Senate. She was appointed in 1922. But she only served one day.

Learn More!

Schatz, Kate, and Miriam Klein Stahl (illust.). *Rad American Women A-Z: Rebels, Trailblazers, and Visionaries Who Shaped Our History ... and Our Future*. San Francisco: City Lights Books, 2015.

Schatz, Kate, and Miriam Klein Stahl (illust.). *Rad Girls Can: Stories of Bold, Brave, and Brilliant Young Women*. New York: Ten Speed Press, 2018.

Shen, Ann. *Bad Girls Throughout History: 100 Remarkable Women Who Changed the World*. San Francisco: Chronicle Books, 2016.

Your Turn!

Now, it's your turn! You get to choose the "Top of the Class: Girl Leader" winner. Who would you pick?

TOP OF THE CLASS: GIRL LEADER

"Top of the Class" means being the best of the best. These prompts will help you think about who'd you pick for the "Top of the Class: Girl Leader" award:

- Why is this person the best "girl leader"? List reasons why this person deserves this award more than others.
- Think about how this person is different from girl leaders in this book. What is special about this person?
- How is this person similar to girl leaders in this book? Describe the qualities that girl leaders should have. How does this person represent those qualities?
- Girl leaders often struggle. They may also face barriers. They're often told they can't do something. They don't run away when things get hard. How does your person overcome challenges?
- Leaders make a lot of decisions. They make tough choices. How is this person a leader?
- Leaders know when to lead. They know when to follow. What does this mean? How does your person do this?
- Leaders have a lot of support. Who helps your person? How does your person treat others?

Consider This!

TAKE A POSITION! Some people think women shouldn't be leaders. Why do you think that is? Do you agree or disagree? Argue your point with reasons and evidence.

SAY WHAT? Are you a leader? Describe your leadership skills. Explain how you want to grow as a leader.

THINK ABOUT IT! Many countries around the world have female leaders. But the United States, Canada, and Mexico are lagging behind. The United States and Mexico have never had a female president. Canada has had only one female prime minister. But she only served for 4 months. What can we do to change this?

Glossary

adapt (uh-DAPT) to change for a new environment

biracial (bye-RAY-shuhl) belonging to two races

composers (kuhm-POH-zurz) people who write music and songs

council (KOUN-suhl) a group of leaders

determined (dih-TUR-mihnd) being focused on goals and not giving up

diplomatic (dip-luh-MAT-ik) being able to solve problems in a friendly way

dynasty (DYE-nuh-stee) a ruling family

emperor (EM-pur-ur) ruler of an empire

labor (LAY-bur) work or employment

orphans (OR-fuhnz) children without parents

persuasive (pur-SWAY-siv) being convincing

politicians (pah-lih-TISH-uhnz) people who serve in the government by being appointed or running for office

prime minister (PRIME MIN-ih-stur) the top leader of a government

warrior (WOR-ee-ur) fighter

Index

45th Parallel Press

Published in the United States of America by Cherry Lake Publishing
Ann Arbor, Michigan
www.cherrylakepublishing.com

Reading Adviser: Marla Conn, MS, Ed., Read-Ability, Inc.
Book Designer: Jen Wahi

Photo Credits: ©Library of Congress/Reproduction No., LC-USZ62-25812, cover (left), 12; ©O'Halloran, Thomas J., photographer/Library of Congress/Reproduction No., LC-DIG-ppmsc-01264, cover (middle), 22; ©Everett Historical/Shutterstock, cover (right), 14; ©Thomas Faull/iStock, 4; ©Historic Images/Alamy Stock Photo, 6; ©Aungkul Intaraprasong/Shutterstock, 8; ©Frye, Thomas, 1710-1762, artist/Library of Congress/Reproduction No., LC-USZ62-115301, 10; ©Library of Congress/Reproduction No., LC-USZ62-105894, 16; ©Sneha Ulhas Lolayekar/Pixtal/age footstock, 18; ©GL Archive / Alamy Stock Photo, 20; ©mark reinstein/Shutterstock, 24; ©Everett – Art/Shutterstock, 26; various art pieces throughout courtesy of Shutterstock

45th Parallel Press is an imprint of Cherry Lake Publishing.

Library of Congress Cataloging-in-Publication Data

Names: Loh-Hagan, Virginia, author.
Title: Girl leaders / by Virginia Loh-Hagan.
Description: [Ann Arbor : Cherry Lake Publishing, 2019] | Series: History's yearbook | Audience: Grade 4 to 6. | Includes bibliographical references and index.
Identifiers: LCCN 2019004193| ISBN 9781534147898 (hardcover) | ISBN 9781534150751 (pbk.) | ISBN 9781534149328 (PDF) | ISBN 9781534152182 (hosted ebook)
Subjects: LCSH: Queens--Biography--Juvenile literature. | Women politicians--Biography--Juvenile literature. | Leadership in women--History--Juvenile literature. | Women heroes--Biography--Juvenile literature.
Classification: LCC D107.3 .L64 2019 | DDC 920.72--dc23
LC record available at https://lccn.loc.gov/2019004193

Printed in the United States of America
Corporate Graphics

About the Author:

Dr. Virginia Loh-Hagan is an author, university professor, former classroom teacher, and curriculum designer. She's a leader too. She leads the Liberal Studies program at San Diego State University. She lives in San Diego with her very tall husband and very naughty dogs. To learn more about her, visit www.virginialoh.com.